The Life

of a

Stone

A. PRINCESS

Archway Publishing books may be ordered through booksellers or by contacting:

Archway Publishing
1663 Liberty Drive
Bloomington, IN 47403
www.archwaypublishing.com
844-669-3957

ISBN: 978-1-6657-5026-4 (sc)
ISBN: 978-1-6657-5136-0 (hc)
ISBN: 978-1-6657-5027-1 (e)

Library of Congress Control Number: 2023917579

Print information available on the last page.

Archway Publishing rev. date: 10/16/2023

The Life

of a

Stone

Prolouge

I am living, I am dying… I love, I forgive, I hate, I feel sorrow, I feel pain… that is the story of my life. Come walk the path of my anguish… Why? Because no one is perfect. Why? because my heart may reach for purity, but I don't think I will ever be there; I shed the shield of pathetic guilt and now, I stand strong as I am. I am who I am, and I show my truest colors. My book is pure, not under the influence. It is me. It is the facts, that I believe are valid. I don't want to fool anyone, I don't want to deceive anyone, I speak the truth. To speak of love and hardship. The pain that I feel is overwhelming, but I still write to feel alive. If you could fathom, grace and love, that is my book. Souls and spirits, intermingled with hope and virtue… Now that: is my book.

Accompany me in this journey, that you will never forget, the love that will never cease to exist. Possess the vortex in your room, where you sleep. That this may be, last time you will wish to do something wrong… Then your wrongs will cease to exist. Your journey of righteousness will start. I will not fail, I will prevail, this is the triumph to our tail! Comeforth, righteousness if you accept it. My life hasn't been all dandy, throughout… poetry has kept me afloat. I thank my avenue and my pieces of paper, that managed to make my mind sharp, all of these years. Fear draped my mind, for so long; today I can say, I am free…

Is this the end? No, it is just the beginning! You found it, whether it is in someone or inside yourself… tattooed marks within your breath, to forever embrace your heart. 100% part of your feelings, that provoke neurotransmitters, chemical impulses. Even if you lost love, and you picked up this book, to see how it felt to reminisce on such a powerful emotion, that is great. I wrote this book for everyone. Those in heartache, it's a journey… Remember me, that's the impact that book holds. A 10 year prelude. Culminating to hold close, to love over and over again; to take on vacation, to work, to school, to smile and cry over! To get that jolt, over that one word or phrase, that shocks your existence.

Bittersweet memories that are relieved over and over. Getting over self hatred, addiction, because of pain… this is your last shot and this book may be it. Well, it is your healing tool. Dark rooms where you loathed existence, here you are… unloading a charge, as the phone rings and you just stare at it, over and over again. The book is on the counter, as if it were an om from the universe, everything might actually be okay. Let me flip to the pages, the poems that talk about anger and self hatred. Here. I. Am. The tears start to pool at the eyes, maybe I don't hate as much as I thought. Phantoms of love start to appear, as you heal…

To feel love and yearning, or feeling whole again with that; therefore, you will never feel little again. That's the goal. Remember my book for ages, let it be timeless. Let it be a beautiful creature that emits as you read!

To those who believed in me,

My mother Marcia Tapia- Reyes, my Queen, the illustrator of the book. Who painted pain into beauty. The woman who would bring me my clothes to different hospitals. The woman who would pick up my phone calls at the hospital everyday. Who would visit me whenever she could. It was a heavy path, 10 years of hospitalizations, away from my mother. Phone calls, just picturing her life away from me. She always received me gracefully. When I left it was always with sorrow. She always had high hopes I would get better…and I did. I love you mom.

My father Damien Castillo Sr, who was there, through every rise and fall gave me the advice only a father can give to a daughter he loves with all his heart.

My brother Damien Castillo Jr, even forgetting about the distance, you will always be my hero; my example and my guide. Since I was a child you always made me smile, when you could find something and I was on duty to find it. Waiting to come home to watch you play video games. How you would yell at the tv. Those were the good days, but now there will be many more.

My sister Dalimar Rodiguez, Even though things transcribed the way that they did. I finally saw how much you loved me. I hope with this book you see how much I love you…

To Rashel Castillo, thank you for being the mother of my nephews.

To Cesar Cadenas, my father in Christ, who always supported me, and never doubted me. Loved me unconditionally… Thank you.

My God mother Daniela Chavez, who always told me to believe in myself, to trust in myself and love in myself.

My aunt Belkis Santana, who is my spiritual guide. Showed me that I could do anything, with the power of God.

My aunt Evelyn Conroy, who visited me in the hospitals when my mom couldn't and always made me smile and laugh, during my phone calls with her.

To my sweet Grandmother Ligia Colon, to the woman who was always by my side and showed me love…

To my sweet Grandmother Ana Josephine Reyes, who motivated me and loved me dearly… rest in peace.

Yolanda Marin, that I have learned to love you like a mother. That has heard me in my woes. For your sweetness, I always felt loved. Love you dearly my mother in Christ.

My Pastors Raymond and Monica Jaques thank you for believing in me, and giving my motherly and fatherly support when she needed it. You both have been my example to continue thus forth. Pastor Raymond your words, yes you can. Pastor Monica thank you for your advice.

Love you both!

What do you do,

When faith is all you have?

Orange is the warmest color…

Hotter than a Supernova!

Yellow Star…

That. Shines so bright;

With all its might! TREMBLING, with words…

Sanctuary of terms.

Fight or Flight?

I feel passionate,

When I vibrate within myself.

Rushing wind,

That propels me forward;

As, I come undone.

Colors of the Earth…

Sorrow that wets the sand.

Blue Sand…

Please dissolve me.

But don't forget;

To erase me completely…

Wreck me.

But destroy me.

Because if, I revive,

You will always make me feel,

Alive…

Breeze, that comes with ease,

Unearth me.

Elixir.

I would wrap the ocean,

Around my finger…

I would string the stars,

Together…

To kiss you.

But I would love you,

As if the Universe never existed.

Big Bang!

Torture.

Eternal Torture without you.

Lust. has become love,

And like powder;

It has dissolved;

TO ARID PAIN!

Candy.

Melancholy abyss…

Why do you look for such torment?

Why not begotten to loves virtue?

So that you may rest in peace.

To death?

Feel my heart,

As it beats for you…

Brightest Star!

MOVE me…

Excite me.

Rise above the horizon.

Sweetness.

Joyous laughter;

Peculiar sunshine!

Cumbersome rise and fall.

Remember happiness;

Remember kindness…

But, remember why you live,

The way you do,

Because that: Is all you have.

Remember me.

As you rose from the underworld,

I rose from my grave.

To meet adjacently so.

We danced in the night as,

The stars twinkled,

Their funny tune.

Embraced our hands,

Together as well as our bodies together,

Thus, to never forget,

Such a moment.

Soulmates...

The woe of agony!

It Was the forthcoming!

You paused and then you left…

Taking my soul, with you.

Remnants of my ashes;

Dispersed in the wind…

As its chime channeled,

My song once more.

Pain!

Fluorescent light,

Vibration of electron,

Photons.

Current that flows from within.

Where have I been?

Locked up in a box:

Where the grandfather clock;

Tick Tocks. Tick. Tocks.

Numb.

Virtue entices faith,

Love entice hope,

Kindness plays its

Playful banter…

Fairly funny with cheeky smiles.

I stood forth before the spectacle;

Humbly so.

You stood with me.

Comforting me in silence.

We cried together in our minds…

Quite the ambiance.

Love filled illusion.

All I see is your silhouette;

I die to relive again.

I know for certain you are with me.

I don't care, if I have to search for you every day!

I am burning,

I just want to feel cool;

My one.

Lingering… I am all in.

As you delicately fade away…

Are you there?

My soul rests in a cell…

Pedals fall, a fall from grace.

My eyes are heavy,

They are closed…

I breath in deeply,

You whisper I love you.

I have never felt so meager.

Passionate self hatred.

I was the victim.

As the pain of death, wept for me.

Agony.

As I walk down the narrow path,

I am awake.

But not forgotten.

Rolling ocean that fills my cavity.

Blue, I am with you.

Walk with me please.

Forget about my broken body,

Forget about my eyes,

Forget about my soul,

Forget about me…

But not my inspiration,

Not my will,

Since that is me.

My will.

Water that Flows,

Beneath the sheet of ice…

Quench my thirst,

Before I freeze.

Warm my frozen soul…

So that I may survive;

So that I may exist:

So that I may revive,

To feel alive.

Melt my soul.

Opaque purple sky,

Velvet white moon.

Come into my room…

Smile at me once more:

To keep me alive again.

A glimpse of hope.

Grey walls white room,

Black table,

Where is my color,

But…

In my eyes.

Where to look?

The smell of pine;

Always forgives the mind!

Leaves have fallen,

Yet sustain their color…

When will the rain stop pouring?

I pour out…

Winter tantric, turbulent sky…

Consume me,

Before I ooze black tar…

Bring forth my essential nectar;

To cleanse my darkness!

COLD.

Heart that beats,

No longer;

Only the echo is heard.

Why should I listen?

Why should I feel?

The wound cuts deep.

But, I do not bleed…

Anguish.

Red roses, bright roses.

Black diamond sky!

Silver stones;

Quite the commotion!

Green evergreen,

Riveting before me…

Remember the words,

For that is my core.

Can you free me?

Blue the Color of tranquility,

Red the color of passion,

Black the color of the possible end?

Blue the color of the ocean,

Red the color of love,

Black the color I know best.

Who am I?

I don't accept dangerous love,

Unless you give it to me!

In my solitude,

Weathered by the seasons.

Feathered trees with leaves,

Bring me the fall...

So that I may flourish!

Come and get me!

Stellar space…
A prelude piece;
That moves with the stars,
Before the horizon:
Before birth!
To be born again!
Rebirth.

Only you can quench my thirst;

Only you can fuel my hunger:

Only you can save me from myself,

Before I self destruct in,

REINCARNATION!

I am back!

Crushed like the souls beneath me…

Aged like the tree before me…

Dressed like the flowers, on the lustrous plants…

When will my demise end?

Fickle uncertainty,

Commencement begins…

Let's begin...

You paused and then you left,

Taking my soul with you!

Tears that cooled my flushed cheeks,

Remind me of better days;

Quiet house,

Quiet room,

Secret smile.

Well, hello.

To cultivate your essence,

Would be a treat:

To see your smile,

Would warm my heart…

But to hold you in my arms,

Would last an eternity!

Hello darling…

Float away with me;

To perplex existence,

Change your internal synopsis:

Precisely so,

Forget about tomorrow,

And remember today,

Since today will be remarkable!

Part of me.

As the music melts away;

The song that I play…

Sharp pieces scatter away.

Tasteful fruit, that encumbers my mouth;

As remnants of you, pronounce themselves,

Once more…

Pieces...

I embrace your heart.

While you hold mine in your hands,

I twirl around, as the wind picks up leaves.

I then remember…

To close my eyes;

You are here.

Don't leave!

The trees danced with the wind,

As you stood before me,

Pensive, perplexed!

Why do you escape my presence?

I am here, we are here…

The present moment. Existence…

Let's dance.

We smiled,

We giggled,

We laughed,

We cried!

It was a glorious day...

Anticipation.

To cultivate your essence,

Would be a treat:

To see your smile,

Would warm my heart…

But to hold you in my arms,

Would last an ETERNITY!

Come and get me.

Jaded Gem, scratch my surface.

Make your sketch on me…

For it is my intense pleasure;

To feel the way you move,

Without being there.

I revolve around you…

You are the center to my space;

A spot in the sky, centers my eyes.

A focus, a moment, a dot, an essence…

Diamond.

I embrace your heart.

While you hold mine,

In your hands…

I twirl around, as the wind picks up leaves.

I then remember, to close my eyes;

You. are. Here.

Hold me.

I was decaying since birth;

Before I met you…

Fire: that now consumes me.

Bring forth, what's alive in me.

I am alive!

The ocean hugs the sand.

As you sparkle more than the stars.

You elude me in my dreams…

…higher than Polaris.

And brighter than its reflection.

Brightest star!

Hunger does not quench my thirst,

For you!

The itch scratches up against my skin,

Like a rough granet!

OVER and OVER again!

Green faded emerald,

Translucent, grey;

Sweet giggle,

Mischievous smile!

Come home to me once more!!

Hunger.

I ache to be in your presence…

Remind me of days;

When the memory of your aura,

Didn't elude me!

Come back.

I cried my soul out for you!

I wept until I couldn't any longer!

Please hold my hand and help me forget!

The cry!

I gasp for air,

As you hold me; Ever so gently…

Caress my heart;

Kiss me in my dreams…

To remind me why I am alive!

The Kiss.

The clock ticks…

As excerpts of time,

Remind me of you;

Oh, how you are missed!

I miss you!

Sparkles that shine around you!

As I recall the night when I first,

Fell for you!

I melted away in my seat,

How could I?

OH, how could I?

Do I?

My heart follows you,

Wherever you go.

Do you feel it because I do!

I love you.

Remnants of autumn fell,

As the budding of the leaves;

Commences a decrescendo,

To a crescendo…

The ice started to melt.

The grass started to grow.

The sun's warmth felt stronger!

Spring is coming soon…

The weeping willow, will not weep because,

Now she will laugh and flourish once more!

Hello Life.

You took my air;

furthermore …

Taking my essence.

Here I am.

Oceanic bodies flow,

Freeform.

To originate back to you.

As I breathe I ache,

Since my heart…

Beats. Only. For. You…

No Air.

I wish you could fathom;

The imprint you've left on me…

I hope that my words,

Caress your eyes;

As your voice touches,

My heart forever and always…

Letters of the heart.

My desire for you,

Burns me like everlasting fire;

That consumes my heart!

Sweet bee produce the honey,

That will sweeten me!

Honey.

Fill my heart with love, As my soul;
Searches for your warmth.,,,

My love.

I crossed the world,

I crossed my life,

I crossed my soul,

To find you…

You are the being that,

That helps me live…

Thank you,

My spirit, that mingles with my soul;

I love you.

The love of my life.

Printed in the United States
by Baker & Taylor Publisher Services